Business Planning *for* Housing

Peter Catterick

Chartered Institute of Housing

The Chartered Institute of Housing

The Chartered Institute of Housing is the professional organisation for all people who work in housing. Its purpose is to take a strategic and leading role in encouraging and promoting the provision of good quality affordable housing for all. The Institute has more than 12,000 members working in local authorities, housing associations, the private sector and educational institutions.

Chartered Institute of Housing
Octavia House
Westwood Way
Coventry CV4 8JP
Telephone: 01203 694433

Business Planning *for* **Housing**

by Peter Catterick

© Chartered Institute of Housing 1995

Published by the Chartered Institute of Housing

ISBN 0 901607 80 0

Graphic design by Henry's House Design Co-operative Ltd.
Printed by Warwick Printing Co. Ltd.

Whilst all reasonable care and attention has been taken in compiling this publication, the publishers regret that they cannot assume liability for any error or omission that it contains.

All rights reserved. No part of this publication may be reproduced, stored in a retrieval system, or transmitted in any form or by any means, electronic, mechanical, photocopying, recording, or otherwise without the prior permission of the publishers.

contents

	About the Author	iv
	Acknowledgements	iv
Chapter 1	**Introduction**	**1**
Chapter 2	**Strategic Management and Business Planning**	**7**
	2.1 Introduction	7
	2.2 Strategic Management	8
	2.3 Corporate Planning	9
	2.4 Business Planning	9
	2.5 The Business Planning Framework	12
	2.6 The Business Planning Process	13
	2.7 What is a Business Plan?	19
	2.8 What Should be in a Business Plan?	20
	2.9 Summary	24
Chapter 3	**Taking Stock**	**31**
	3.1 Introduction	31
	3.2 Stakeholders	32
	3.3 External Analysis	33
	3.4 Internal Analysis	37
	3.5 Summary	43
Chapter 4	**Objectives and Strategies**	**47**
	4.1 Introduction	47
	4.2 Setting Objectives	49
	4.3 Charactersistics of Objectives	52
	4.4 Selecting Strategies	53
	4.5 Setting Objectives and Strategies – the Process	56
	4.6 Structure of Strategies	59
Chapter 5	**Finance**	**61**
	5.1 Introduction	61
	5.2 Financial Accounting and Management Accounting	63
	5.3 Main Financial Statements	64
	5.4 Cost Accounting	71
	5.5 Summary	73

Chapter 6	**Performance Review and Staff Appraisal**	**74**
	6.1 Introduction	74
	6.2 Performance Review	75
	6.3 Structure	75
	6.4 Effectiveness	76
	6.5 Individual Appraisal	78
	6.6 Performance Indicators	80
	6.7 Links with Other Issues	82
	6.8 Summary	84
	Sources of Information	**85**
	Further Reading	

case studies

Chapter 1
1. Benefits of Business Planning – *Devon & Cornwall HA* — 3
2. Business Planning & CCT – *Oldham MBC* — 4

Chapter 2
3. Background to Business Planning Process – *Lewisham LBC* — 10
4. Business Planning Process – *Charnwood Forest HA* — 14
5. Business Planning Process – *Lewisham LBC* — 18
6. Contents of a Business Plan – *Devon & Cornwall HA* — 24
7. Business Planning – *Leeds City Council* — 26
8. Business Planning Process – *English Churches Housing Group* — 28

Chapter 3
9. Examining the Current Position – *Northern Counties HA* — 42

Chapter 4
10. Objectives and Strategies – *Charnwood Forest HA* — 48
11. Co-ordinating Activities – *English Churches Housing Group* — 50
12. Planning Care Services – *East Dorset HA* — 57
13. Introducing Business Planning – *Warwick DC* — 58
14. Gaining Commitment – *Lewisham LBC* — 59

Chapter 5
15. Financial Planning – *English Churches Housing Group* — 62
16. Financial Planning – *Devon & Cornwall HA* — 64

Chapter 6
17. Performance Review – *Charnwood Forest HA* — 77
18. The Review Process – *Lewisham LBC* — 78
19. Links with Other Issues – *Lewisham LBC* — 82

About the Author

Peter Catterick worked for a property development company, a housing association and in local authority housing before joining the Audit Commission. He is a member of both the Chartered Institute of Housing and the Royal Institution of Chartered Surveyors and has a masters degree in business administration. As manager at the Audit Commission's northern region project unit, Peter has reviewed business planning, performance management and quality improvement in numerous public sector organisations.

Peter Catterick is also author of *Total Quality – An Introduction to Quality Management in Social Housing* (CIH 1992)

Acknowledgements

Whilst accepting responsibility for any errors or omissions in the text, the author acknowledges the contribution, in various ways, of the following people and would like to thank them for their input to this publication:

Colin Ball	*Charnwood Forest Housing Association*
Lisa Burns	*Northern Counties Housing Association*
Teresa Butcher	*Devon and Cornwall Housing Association*
Kevin Dey	*East Dorset Housing Association*
Derek Dyas	*Warwick District Council*
Ashley Hook	*London Borough of Lewisham*
Tony Lightfoot	*Havelok Housing Association*
Jason McGilp	*Priority Estates Project*
Andrew Oates	*Oldham Metropolitan District Council*
Jon Passmore	*Moat Housing Society*
Bill Payne	*Yorkshire Metropolitan Housing Association*
John Perry	*Chartered Institute of Housing*
Simon Rose	*SJC Rose and Associates*
Gwen Smith	*Leeds City Council*
Caroline Smith	*English Churches Housing Group*

The text does not necessarily represent the views of the author's employer.

chapter 1

Introduction

This chapter:
- identifies who this book is aimed at
- introduces business planning
- outlines subsequent chapters.

By the end of this chapter the reader should:
- understand that business planning is an approach developed in the private sector which can be applied to social housing
- know what the following chapters are about.

There are many detailed texts on business planning. This book is designed to provide an additional and easily accessible source of information specifically for housing practitioners and housing students. It is intended to clarify some of the confusion which exists about the introduction of business planning in social housing.

The introduction of Compulsory Competitive Tendering (CCT) in local authority housing, the reduction in grant rates for housing associations and the possibility of local housing companies have changed the environment in which social housing is obliged to operate. Business planning is one of many tools and techniques which are being introduced to assist housing organisations to operate in a competitive culture.

Business Planning for Housing

The majority of housing practitioners, choose housing as a career because they are attracted by a public service ethos, not a profit ethos. Nevertheless, housing practitioners need to be aware of the techniques being applied to bring about a more business like approach in social housing.

Business planning is a technique which was primarily developed for the private sector often as a method of attracting financial support. It is however already being used in a number of public sector organisations. When used successfully business planning provides a method of co-ordinating and directing an organisation's skills and resources to focus on the challenges facing the organisation.

Business planning actually combines a number of practices which are already in existence such as budget setting, quality improvement initiatives, tenant consultation and performance appraisal. Business planning should not be seen as distinct from existing planning processes such as the Housing Investment Programme, Housing Management Plans (in Scotland) and Housing Corporation requirements for housing associations.

Business Planning: Why do it?

"If you don't know where you are and where you want to go, how can you ever hope to get anywhere?

"Business planning is a method of keeping in touch with tenants and corporate customers: it provides a methodology for working with them to deliver improvements in the service the association provides.

"For staff, business planning provides a way of focussing on the importance of customers and customer satisfaction and forms a way of achieving involvement in the decision making process.

"In all, business planning leads to improved service delivery and better productivity. It is a way of strengthening the organisation to survive and thrive in the future."

Colin Ball   *Chief Executive, Charnwood Forest Housing Association*

Chapter 1 • Introduction

A business plan provides a method of integrating the many aspects of running a housing service. It is a statement of what the organisation wants to achieve and how it seeks to achieve it. It is a management tool for directing action and monitoring progress.

Be aware, however, that the introduction of business planning will require time and effort which may not provide immediate benefits. The temptation to delay starting because of current pressures should be avoided.

For many people business planning will be seen as an unwelcome addition to the management of social housing. Criticism from some is to be expected. It is incumbent on senior managers, responsible for introducing business planning, to ensure that staff, committee members and tenants are informed about why it is being introduced, what it is for and how every one will be involved.

Benefits of Business Planning – *Devon and Cornwall Housing Association*

Business planning has enabled committee members and staff to know and understand each other much better. For both groups, joint working on the planning process has provided strong 'ownership' of the resulting business plan.

Devon and Cornwall's business plan was well received by private lenders who were able to acknowledge that the association is confident about where it is going, is sensible in its decision making and is aware of the complexities of the environment in which it is operating.

A common criticism is that because many of the factors affecting social housing are different from those faced in private sector organisations, business planning will not be of use. In fact many private sector organisations face complicated problems such as low investment, poor infra-structure and adverse economic conditions. The distinction between 'public' and 'private' sectors is becoming less clear and in any case, the more complex the situation, the greater is the need to plan.

Some Myths about Business Planning

"Business planning is only for senior executives !"

"Business plans can only be written by experts !"

"It is possible to write a perfect business plan !"

"Business planning won't work in the public sector !"

There are often political sensitivities about the use of the term 'business' and the use of other terminology which was formerly associated only with commercial organisations. The terminology used may initially be off-putting to housing practitioners. There is no problem or detriment in using terms such as 'service planning' or 'service delivery planning'. The issues are the same and the benefits should not be lost because of concerns about terminology.

Compulsory Competitive Tendering provides further impetus for developing business planning. It means that local authority housing departments will require separate business plans for their client and contractor roles. The following chapters describe an approach to business planning which applies to both the client and contractor functions although the emphasis may be different in some places. The approach described can also be adapted for use within resident-led organisations such as co-operatives and Estate Management Boards.

Business Planning and CCT — *Oldham MBC*

Oldham MBC Housing Department's Management Division's business plan developed over a 12 month period largely as a response to the introduction of CCT for housing management. The aim of the first plan was to:

- clarify, for staff, the role of the divsion under CCT

- demonstrate, to the client, the contractor's ability to deliver a quality housing service.

Chapter 1 • Introduction

The introduction of business planning at Oldham has had the immediate benefit of enabling staff to see where the organisation is going and how any proposed changes will affect them. Prior to the establishment of the business plan it was felt that although managers were aware of the direction the department was taking, particularly in response to CCT, the majority of staff did not share this clarity about all the issues confronting the department.

The department considers that the benefits which have accrued for staff will be extended to customers because business planning has helped to: develop the organisational structure, introduce improved procedures and increase the performance of both directly employed staff and sub-contractors.

Developing a business plan has encouraged a team approach to helping the organisation to clearly prioritise its work and channel resources into meeting the objectives identified were identified.

Structure of Following Chapters

In the following chapters business planning is described as a continuous process involving: setting of objectives, determining a way of meeting those objectives and reviewing performance. Chapter two provides an overview of business planning. Chapters three to six provide further detail of how you can develop a business plan relevant to your own organisation.

Each chapter is illustrated by case study examples from local authorities and housing associations which have provided information based on their own experiences of business planning.

Chapter 2 describes the business planning cycle and suggests the likely contents of a business plan. The chapter provides an overall summary of the role and nature of business planning.

Chapter 3 suggests that the rapidly changing environment in which social housing operates requires organisations to have a structured way of considering all the factors which affect them. It considers the issues which will need to be addressed at the start of the business planning process and which will form the basis for decisions about future services and the way they are provided.

Chapter 4 considers how to go about setting objectives and developing strategies to meet them. The results of the exercise described at Chapter

3 will inform your organisation about where it is heading. Setting objectives provides clarity about what needs to be done to meet the challenges facing the organisation. The chapter shows that personal and team objectives must be linked with departmental and corporate objectives to provide co-ordination throughout the organisation

Having decided what its objectives are, your organisation will then be faced with determining how best to meet those objectives. There are a number of options available to local authorities and housing associations. Clarifying objectives and alternative strategies provides an opportunity for thorough review of existing arrangements.

Chapter 5 highlights that setting objectives and developing strategies to meet those objectives will have financial implications. Expert financial assistance will be required to ensure that your business plan is backed by sound financial data. This chapter provides an outline of the financial aspects of developing a business plan. It includes examples of the main financial statements which are included in a business plan and an explanation of them.

Chapter 6 considers how plans should be monitored and reviewed. Performance review may initially be seen as the link which completes the business planning cycle. In fact it also provides information about the direction the organisation should take in the future.

Chapter 2

Strategic Management & Business Planning

This chapter:
- describes strategic management and business planning
- describes the business planning cycle
- summarises the likely contents of a business plan.

By the end of this chapter the reader should:
- understand the concept of strategic management
- know what a business plan is
- understand the business planning process
- be aware of the likely framework of a business plan.

2.1 Introduction

"Business planning", "strategic management", "corporate policy" are all terms used to describe the study of the way organisations analyse their position and consider their way forward. There are numerous variations in the terminology. It is important to understand the terminology but not to become pre-occupied with it.

2.2 Strategic Management

Strategic Management is that part of the management function which relates to the direction the organisation should take. It is about how to bring together all the elements of the organisation and how best to harness those elements in a way which will maximise their potential.

Strategic management in a local authority is concerned with such issues as:

- whether to run a housing management Direct Service Organisation (DSO)
- whether to enter into a large scale voluntary transfer

In a housing association examples of strategic management are:

- whether to merge with another association
- whether to bid for housing management CCT contracts.

The nature of strategic management is quite different from the management processes which the majority of staff will usually be involved with. The majority of staff in a local authority or housing association are involved in operational activities. Strategic decision making is concerned with the future direction of the organisation and therefore has implications for all other aspects of the management of the organisation and its sub units. Strategic management leads operational management.

Strategic management is about matching an organisation's activities to the environment in which it operates. It is therefore extremely important to have a framework to analyse that environment and thereby consider how to respond.

There is little chance of taking advantage of opportunities if the resources in an organisation are insufficient to do so. Strategic management must take account of resource implications. In effect it is the decision making process which maps out the route of where an organisation should go and how to get there.

Strategic decisions are inseparable from the values and culture of the organisation in which they are made. Strategic decisions are based on the existing culture and play a large part in shaping the future culture.

Chapter 2 • Strategic Management and Business Planning

> **Strategic Decisions**
>
> - respond to current and impending changes in the environment
>
> - are medium to long term in their consequences
>
> - affect future prioritisation of resources

2.3   Corporate Planning

Corporate planning relates to the whole organisation i.e. the entire corporate entity. Therefore in local authority housing it would be inappropriate to use this term because the corporate entity is the sum of all local authority services.

Whilst a local authority may have a corporate plan a single department or directorate cannot. Likewise, in a housing association corporate planning is an appropriate term to use where the planning process relates to the entire association rather than a single area of activity.

Corporate planning consists of guiding statements about the long term future of the organisation. In social housing decisions are necessarily restricted by the nature of the organisation and the statutory regime under which it operates. This is a notable difference from the private sector in which the primary purpose of the organisation is to make a profit rather than to provide specific services.

For the purpose of this text corporate planning is the decision making and planning processes undertaken by elected members, voluntary committee members and senior management. It determines the key aspects of the future direction of the organisation. This accepts as pre-determined that the service is social housing.

2.4   Business Planning

Business planning is probably now the most frequently used term to describe any form of organisational planning although a number of public sector organisations prefer to use terms such as "service planning" usually for political reasons. Business planning is not necessarily planning for the entire organisation. Therefore the development section of a housing association or the contractor function of a local authority may have a business plan. It is however to be hoped that such plans have been formulated in consultation with and integrated with the other functions of the organisation i.e. that they feed into the corporate plan and support the implementation of the corporate plan.

Corporate planning should be part of the strategic management of an organisation. Business planning is a "sub-set" of corporate planning.

The Planning Pyramid

The different levels of planning must be inter-related

figure 2.1 the Planning Pyramid

Background to Business Planning — *Lewisham LBC*

Business planning is not new to Lewisham. There has been much debate about the appropriateness of using private sector terminology in a public service organisation and term 'Service Planning' is often used instead.

A system of service planning has existed for five years and the process has evolved into a systematic business planning framework. In 1993 the organisation invested in two days training for all managers.

Chapter 2 • Strategic Management and Business Planning

The process operates on two levels ; a departmental plan and individual service unit plans. The term 'Service Unit' refers to each identifiable business unit such as the Homeless Persons' Unit, Neighbourhood Offices, the Personnel and Training Section etc. Service Unit plans support the departmental plan. In preparation for CCT, the structure has recently been developed to establish a DSO Business Plan containing all the key financial and resource planning for the emerging contractor units which will form the DSO.

Business Planning for Housing

Glossary

To avoid further confusion about the terminology used in this text the glossary below sets out the main definitions which will be used.

Term	Definition	Explanation
Mission Statement	A vision of what the organisation wants to move towards. Summary of the organisation's core purpose. A motivating statement.	A sentence or two which sums–up the purpose of the organisation and which demonstrates this to any one associated with or interested in the organisation.
Policy	The guidelines which set out the way in which the organisation will go about achieving its mission statement. A set of principles which the organisation will adhere to in its internal and external relationships.	The overarching principles set by elected members or committee members. An organisation's policies determine what it will and will not do. They thereby form the foundation of objectives and strategies.
Objectives	The place at which the organisation or business unit wants to be in relation to its activities.	An objective sets a standard against which performance can be assessed. Should set out clearly what the organisation or business unit wants to achieve and by when. Should be specific, measurable, achievable, realistic, timed.

continued over...

Chapter 2 • Strategic Management and Business Planning

Strategy	What will be done to achieve objectives. How resources will be deployed.	Objectives can usually be achieved in a number of ways. The strategy an organisation or business unit takes is the approach it will adopt to achieve its objectives.
Corporate Plan	Plan for the entire organisation.	Must give direction to the business plans which will support it.
Business or Service Plans	Plans containing the objectives and strategies for the service. These should draw together the objectives & strategies of a number of sub–units or business units.	Must give direction to the plans of the business units which in turn must support the business plan for the whole service.
Business unit / Service unit / Section Plan	Plans for an identifiable Unit or Section.	Support the service plan and set the framework for action plans.
Action Plans	Plans containing the detail of the strategy. Plans which clarify the required input from the teams and individuals of which the organisation is comprised.	Translate strategies into a series of steps which taken sequentially will move the organisation towards its objectives.
Monitoring	The review process. Feedback information.	Evaluation of past and current performance and the starting point for further objective setting and strategies. Gathering feedback information in order to evaluate successes and areas for improvement in the future.

2.5 The Business Planning Framework

Business planning is a process of assessing an organisation's position, determining where it wants to be, considering how it will get there and reviewing progress.

The process can be divided into five basic questions:

	Question	Requirement
1	**What is our Purpose?**	Analysis of the component parts of the organisation and who they work for. A clear understanding of the needs of "customers" (internal and external).
2	**Where are we now?**	Intelligence gathering and analysis on the environment in which the organisation operates. Consideration of the external threats and opportunities which exist and of internal strengths and weaknesses. Review of the recent and current performance of the organisation and projection of those trends.
3	**Where do we want to be?**	Consideration of the views of all interested parties e.g. tenants, staff, DoE/Housing Corporation Establishment of the factors critical for the organisation's success. Comparison of the aims within the organisation and the desires of those for whom services are provided. Consideration of any conflicting aims. Market research and consultation to confirm objectives.
4	**How are we going to get there?**	Establishment of the strategy which will be adopted to meet the aims which have been confirmed.

continued over...

Chapter 2 • Strategic Management and Business Planning

	Question	Requirement
		Decisions about future actions to minimise threats and weaknesses and maximise on opportunities and strengths. Forecasts about expected outcomes and financial consequences. Action plans nominating responsibilities and time scales.
5	**How will we know whether we are getting there?**	Monitoring at all levels of the organisation to review progress towards objectives.

2.6 The Business Planning Process

Business planning is a cyclical process. It should start with an examination of what the organisation is about. Business plans should be linked to a corporate plan. In line with the framework above, this enables the creation of action plans and individual performance targets which in turn are monitored to inform the revision of the business plan. This in turn informs the revision of the corporate plan.

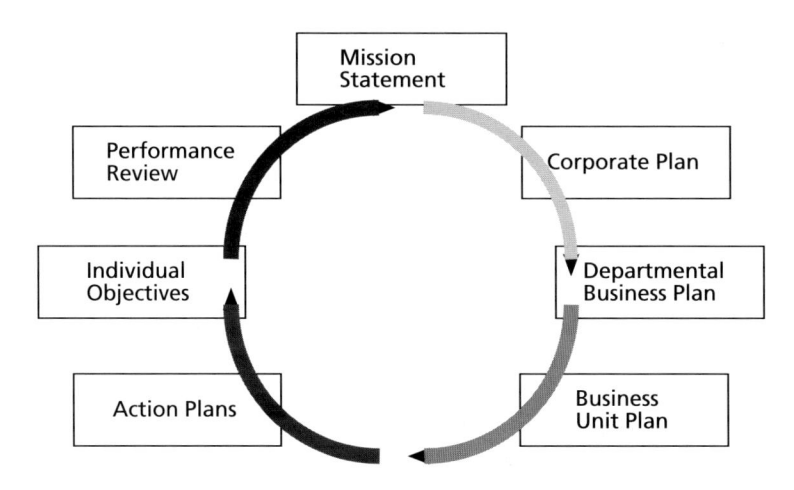

figure 2.2 Business planning is a cyclical process

15

Business Planning for Housing

Although business planning is concerned with organisational development and progress, the organisation is the sum of a number of component parts. Organisations can only advance by taking specific action in respect of each of those components.

Business Planning Process — *Charnwood Forest Housing Association*

Business planning is viewed as integral to all that the association does. It is seen as part of a process of continual improvement in service quality which involves the association's committee members, staff, tenants and 'corporate customers'.

The process began at the Association's first committee/staff review weekend in 1993 which is now called the 'Back to the Future Weekend'. The cycle now operates annually as set out below:

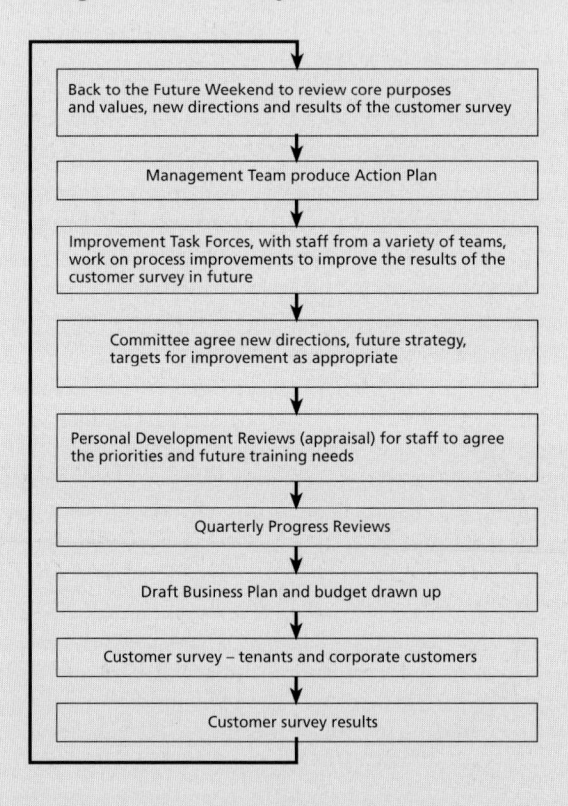

```
┌──────────────────────────────────────────────────────────────┐
│                                                              │
│   Back to the Future Weekend to review core purposes         │
│   and values, new directions and results of the customer survey │
│                           ↓                                  │
│         Management Team produce Action Plan                  │
│                           ↓                                  │
│   Improvement Task Forces, with staff from a variety of teams, │
│   work on process improvements to improve the results of the │
│   customer survey in future                                  │
│                           ↓                                  │
│   Committee agree new directions, future strategy,           │
│   targets for improvement as appropriate                     │
│                           ↓                                  │
│   Personal Development Reviews (appraisal) for staff to agree│
│   the priorities and future training needs                   │
│                           ↓                                  │
│              Quarterly Progress Reviews                      │
│                           ↓                                  │
│        Draft Business Plan and budget drawn up               │
│                           ↓                                  │
│     Customer survey – tenants and corporate customers        │
│                           ↓                                  │
│                Customer survey results                       │
│                                                              │
└──────────────────────────────────────────────────────────────┘
```

To build on this continual improvement process, the association holds regular tenants' meetings for all its estates to improve feedback. It also

Chapter 2 • Strategic Management and Business Planning

holds regular staff briefing sessions and is currently completing a programme to reach the Investors in People standard. Staff skills are being developed in financial planning and a range of quality improvement techniques to ensure that work practices improve to deliver the aims of Charnwood Forest's business plan as cost effectively as possible.

To achieve effective business planning requires commitment and extensive investment in time. To instigate the process and sustain it requires:

- understanding at all levels
- training at all levels
- the involvement and ownership of staff
- additional / external support in the areas where staff do not have sufficient skills or expertise;
- perseverance: it will not come right in one annual cycle.

Business planning is not just about writing a document.

The document is:

- the product of a process of considering what the organisation is going to do

- clarification for all vested interests of where they fit in

- the framework by which the organisation can assess its progress as it goes through the year (or other period for which the plan applies)

- a baseline from which to consider amendments to future plans.

Business Planning Process – *Lewisham LBC*

The departmental plan is drafted by a selection of key managers representing different interests across the department. The lead person for the process is the Director of Housing. The brainstorming process to determine strategic objectives takes place at an 'away day' meeting. The draft plan is made available to all managers for consideration and contribution.

The draft plan is then subject to extensive consultation with all 17 Neighbourhood Committees, five Area Forums and Lewisham Tenants Council before finally being considered by the Housing Committee.

As the process has developed it has been refined to ensure that customers can actively input to the process and are not just presented with a plan with little opportunity to alter the content. In 1994 a video was produced to aid this process and also to present the main themes of the Business Plan to all staff. All staff and tenant representatives receive a copy of the plan and a summary is also produced for distribution to other stakeholders.

Following agreement of the departmental plan, all Service Units then develop their own Business Plans in conjunction with customers. In the case of Neighbourhoods, , this is undertaken through Neighbourhood Committees. Support Service Units are required to develop their Business Plans in consultation with internal stakeholders i.e. operational Service Units and service users. Service Unit Plans are developed by all staff, usually at 'away days'. Each Service Unit negotiates its contribution to departmental objectives with the centre. For example, on rent arrears it would be expected that a Neighbourhood's contribution to the departmental objective would reflect historic performance, the debt profile, current resourcing, anticipated productivity etc. not just a pro rata apportionment of the overall objective. In this way, Service Unit Plans are made challenging whilst being achievable.

The Lewisham approach provides a process in which the determination of the over-arching objectives is senior management driven. The objectives are achieved by developing strategies in a bottom-up manner. In essence it is the responsibility of each team to decide upon the processes it will perform to meet the required outcomes. This allows ownership to rest with the people who will implement the plans.

Chapter 2 • **Strategic Management and Business Planning**

2.7 What is a Business Plan?

The process of business planning is as important as the resulting document in effecting change. Nevertheless, it is easier to embark on the process if you have in mind what might be produced.

A business plan is the document which shows how an organisation proposes to put its strategic planning into effect.

Business Plans – The basic questions

Question	Answered By:
What is our purpose?	Mission Statement
Where are we now?	Candid analysis of Strengths, Weaknesses, Opportunities and Threats
Where do we want to be?	Clear objectives
How do we get there?	Establishing priorities and strategies
How will we know that we are getting there?	Effective monitoring and appraisal

---

A business plan should not be a document produced by the senior management team without the involvement of the staff who will be charged with the responsibility of putting it into effect.

A business plan should be the representation of the consensus of the organisation. Staff at all levels need to "own" the business plan if there is to be hope that it will be an effective tool for organisational development and progress.

A business plan is therefore a summary of the planning process in the first instance and is subsequently a starting point for the annual planning process.

The plan should be in a format which will enable it to be used as a working tool throughout the year:

Business Planning for Housing

- to assess progress
- to highlight problems
- to provide a benchmark for revising objectives where necessary.

Remember, it is not written in tablets of stone. If issues affecting the organisation change, the plan must change to recognise that. It must not become a straight-jacket.

A business plan has a variety of uses. Some are:

- to clarify direction
- to set priorities
- to assign responsibilities
- to inform budget setting
- to demonstrate change
- to attract additional investment
- to strengthen performance management.

The variety of reasons for producing a business plan means that there cannot be a common template applicable to all organisations.

Some of the information may be so sensitive that in a competitive environment it would be inappropriate to let it become public information. It is common practice in many organisations to hold two plans: one for internal use only and one for public information.

2.8   What Should be in a Business Plan?

Most business plans set out some information about the organisation. This very often includes some history of the development of the organisation or important decisions which were taken which have a bearing on present circumstances.

Some facts and figures which are commonly included in local authority or housing association business plans are:

- size and value of housing stock
- number and type of consumer groups
- number of staff and organisational structure
- summary of capital and revenue estimates
- assumptions about interest rates, inflation and other variable costs

The body of a plan for a housing association or local authority housing department should:

Chapter 2 • Strategic Management and Business Planning

1. summarise its purpose
2. demonstrate its consideration of the various elements of its environment
3. provide a rationale for the decisions about the impact of those elements on the organisation and set objectives
4. show how it seeks to meet those objectives
5. demonstrate its financial capability to implement its strategy
6. provide time scales and nominate responsibility.

1 Consider your Purpose

Undertaking a function i.e. that of providing or enabling the provision social housing is not necessarily the same as meeting a purpose:

- function is about *input* (what you do)
- purpose is about *outcome* (what you achieve)

Your purpose must be outcome based if it is to satisfy your consumers' needs.

Without giving adequate consideration to what the organisation is in existence to achieve, it is likely that inputs are not geared to meet the desired outcomes. In this case the work of the department or association continues without focus and without co-ordination between different sections or units. This was the old image of public sector bureaucracy in which systems suited staff needs and consumers had to adapt accordingly.

The purpose of a social housing organisation is more prescribed than that of a private sector business. Nevertheless, for the reasons stated above, purpose should be analysed and clarified. For example:

- is it part of the association's purpose to expand its housing stock?
- is it part of the local authority's purpose to directly provide social housing?

Examination of purpose may challenge the assumptions of many staff. This in itself is a useful exercise.

To consider its purpose, an organisation must work backwards from its usual perspective. The question "What is our purpose" i.e. what do we want to achieve must be answered in respect of the various stakeholders to whom the organisation relates. Stakeholders are any one or any group

Business Planning for Housing

which has a vested interest in what your organisation does. This notion is pursued in Chapter Three.

Mission Statement

The function of a mission statement is to summarise the purpose of an organisation.

The mission statement cannot encompass everything. It should provide a succinct summary of what the organisation is about and should be a point of reference or focus as the organisation develops its consideration of its purpose. If, after more detailed analysis at a later stage in the planning process, it becomes apparent that the purpose of the organisation is not that which was first thought, the mission statement can be changed.

The purpose of the organisation must be kept in mind as the planning process progresses.

Some examples of mission statements are shown below:

> "To be a caring provider of quality social housing, maintaining a solid financial base and striving for excellence in everything we do"
> (Havelok Housing Association)

> "To meet the locally identified needs in the communities we serve, providing and maintaining suitable, high quality, affordable homes and giving continuing support to residents"
> (Charnwood Forest Housing Association)

> "To deliver an effective, efficient, accessible, comprehensive housing service which is sensitive to the needs of users and providers and which has regard to quality and equity at all times".
> (Leeds City Council)

Unless action is co-ordinated in a way which will allow the organisation to work towards it, the mission statement becomes hollow and meaningless.

It is essential if such statements are to mean anything that they can be extended to provide quantifiable objectives and that practical strategies can be implemented to achieve the objectives.

2 Consider the Factors Which Affect You – Present and Future

Management text books talk in grand terms about environmental analysis. This means that business planning requires organisations to consider all the factors which affect the organisation.

Such factors may be from outside the organisation e.g. changes to legislation, reductions in funding allocations, or from within e.g. staffing issues.

Because competition has traditionally been limited or even non existent in social housing, it has not been necessary to consider, in detail, the factors which will affect future services. This situation no longer applies.

External Analysis

External change is one of the major influences on any organisation. For some organisations the environment is more turbulent than others. Of course the environment has always shaped the way local authorities and housing associations provide services. The difference is that to be able to recognise and analyse these factors in a structured way provides a method of being better able to respond to them.

Business planning methodology has traditionally grouped environmental analysis under the following headings (sometimes called PEST analysis):

- Political and governmental environment
- Economic environment
- Social/cultural environment
- Technological environment

Each of these is dealt with in more detail in Chapter Three.

Internal Analysis

This is an analysis of the factors within the organisation and the resources available to it. This must be open and honest. If it is not it will not add value to the process.

Issues to consider are:

- current levels of service
- staffing levels, staff skills and abilities
- training needs
- office location / structure
- financial position
- costs – staff and non–staff.

Each of these is dealt with in more detail in Chapter Three.

3 Set the objectives you want to meet

Having read your business plan the reader should be clear about the key objectives for the organisation as a whole and the primary objectives for each section of the organisation.

To achieve effective benefits through business planning you need to make objectives specific and measurable and within reach or they will become demotivating.

A business plan which contains only vague or imprecise objectives cannot be used as a working tool.

A starting point for defining and prioritising objectives is to consider the critical success factors for your housing department or housing association. Critical success factors are those things which you must achieve to maintain and improve your position. Some examples may be:

- to successfully achieve a given level of private investment
- to win housing management CCT contracts
- to achieve a large scale voluntary transfer by a set date.

Carefully defining objectives in relation to the critical success factors which the organisation is seeking to meet is the way to turn business planning into a practical exercise rather than a public relations exercise.

4 Outline a strategy to meet those objectives

This is vital. The terms strategy and objective are often interchanged and confused (see glossary in chapter 2).

- an objective is what you want to achieve
- a strategy is how you propose to achieve it.

Having looked at the areas in which you are strong or weak you will be better able to take decisions about the most appropriate ways of achieving your objectives.

In the areas where you have strengths you may wish to concentrate or develop. In the areas where you are weak you may decide to address those weaknesses with a view to developing opportunities or you may wish to put those areas to one side and leave them to other housing organisations.

Chapter 2 • Strategic Management and Business Planning

- introducing a programme of performance review and personal development plans and working towards 'Investors in People' accreditation

- devising service standards, policy and procedure manuals and performance indicators

- integrating the measures above into contract area service plans in consultation with tenants

- establishing a programme of quality audits to review service developments.

Benefits

Establishing business plans has provided a way for the housing departments to:

- state clearly how services will be delivered to meet explicit objectives

- provide a framework for performance management.

For Leeds City Council, an authority which is committed to maintaining a successful DSO under CCT, business planning has aided the run up to competition by:

- establishing the capability of the DSO and conveying this to the client side and to tenants

- providing a thorough review of financial and other resources and how they are deployed

- demonstrating to staff and tenants that the DSO has a well thought through approach to competing in a competitive environment

- assisting the culture change required for competition

Business Planning Process — *English Churches Housing Group*

English Churches Housing Group is a diverse and dispersed organisation. Staff and committee members were involved in the planning process to achieve a plan to which the whole organisation felt committed. ECHG's first corporate plan was developed in 1992.

A planning team was set up, comprising committee members, senior staff and middle managers. An external consultant was used as a facilitator. The planning team followed through the whole process until the plan was adopted by the National Committee of ECHG.

Consultation involved a number of processes including a SWOT analysis which involved all staff and committee members. This was followed by full consultation on the first draft of the corporate objectives and strategies. The results were fed back into the final draft which was discussed at a Committee residential conference involving members of the National Committee, Regional Committees and the planning team. This was followed by a 'roadshow' of presentations to all staff and to the Tenants Conference.

The objectives are set out in ECHG's Business Plan which is reviewed annually. It sets out the association's three year strategies and five year financial planning. Performance targets for the various aspects of the business plan are set on a bottom–up approach thereby achieving a two way approach to planning.

Chapter 3

Taking Stock

This chapter:
- provides a framework for systematically analysing external factors affecting your organisation.
- suggests a way of appraising the capability and resources available to your organisation.

By the end of this chapter the reader should:
- be able to analyse the external environment
- be able to assess their own organisation's ability to meet the challenges posed by its changing environment.

3.1 Introduction

This chapter is about addressing the part of the business planning framework which asks; *"Where are we now?"*

Before your local authority or housing association is able to make objective decisions about its way forward it must take stock of its current situation and the factors which are likely to affect it in the future. It must also consider its capability to deal with the factors which affect the way it works.

Business Planning for Housing

The factors affecting social housing are considerable and complex. A logical approach is required to analyse the environment. Similarly, organisations need a framework to appraise their resources and capabilities. Comparing both of these provides a basis for setting objectives and developing strategies for meeting those objectives.

3.2   Stakeholders

Every one who comes into contact with a housing association or local housing authority housing department or has a relationship with one in some way is a stakeholder i.e. has a stake in it.

Stakeholders are the people who have a vested interest in an organisation.

Some of these are:

- tenants
- prospective tenants
- local communities (regardless of type of tenure)
- elected members
- staff
- unions
- government agencies
- funding and regulatory bodies
- local authorities (in the case of housing associations)
- housing associations (in the case of local authorities)

If there is not already an adequate mechanism for your organisation to consult its stakeholders this should be rectified as a priority.

Think about what the various stakeholders want from the organisation:

- what are their objectives?
- do they have different priorities?
- do their objectives and priorities conflict with each other?

A compromise will be inevitable. But you must decide on this 'trade-off' position for yourself and you must be clear within your organisation about the position in relation to each stakeholder group.

3.3 External Analysis

The environment in which any organisation operates is largely outside its control. Despite this it is important that due consideration is given to the elements which affect the organisation.

The purpose of environmental analysis is twofold:

- to collect information to understand trends
- to isolate the factors which will affect the organisation.

Chapter Two suggested a number of headings under which external factors can be assessed.

Give consideration to each of these at the start of your planning process but remember; not all will have equal importance all the time. The following framework based on political, economic, social and technological factors is often called a PEST analysis.

Political and Governmental Environment

Your planning process should expand this heading. You will need to ask:

- What is the current governments attitude towards social housing? Is it likely to change?
- Is the government likely to change and will a new government have a significantly different approach?
- What legislation is affecting you and will affect you in the future? For example community care, creation of local housing companies, CCT?
- What about the European Community and the European Parliament? What are their likely affects on you?

In some cases you will be aware of decisions taken or announcements made about likely decisions in the future. Gather together the information you have and your considered opinion about future trends. For each government agency in your list ask:

- what are the key factors?
- how will these affect your organisation?

Provide a documented summary for consultation inside and outside your organisation.

Your list under this heading may for example include:

Business Planning for Housing

- Department of the Environment
- Housing Corporation
- Welsh Office
- Scottish Office
- Scottish Homes
- Benefits Agency
- Department of Social Security
- Health and Safety Executive
- European Parliament

Who are your competitors and how will they be affected by such factors?

Again many of these will be unknown. Assumptions should be made and attention given to them on the basis of:

- the likelihood of them happening
- the risk they present to your organisation.

Prioritise actions in respect of assumptions with high likelihood and high risk.

Economic Environment

The economic situation of those in housing need is an issue which has been under debate for a long time by all those involved in social housing.

Business planning is unlikely to bring anything new to the debate. It will however provide the opportunity to focus economic issues in relation to your organisation, your tenants and your other stakeholders.

You will need to ask, for example:

- What is likely to happen to interest rates and inflation?
- What is the likely future trend in disposable income for your tenants and future tenants?
- What do you think will happen to grant rates and what effect will this have on future rent levels?
- Is there any way capital can be released for investment, under existing arrangements? Under new arrangements?

Socio-cultural Environment

Social factors are well known to housing staff as being of fundamental importance in service delivery. They are just as important in business planning.

Many of the social difficulties which a local authority or housing association is aware of or anticipates are intractable. Nevertheless the planning process requires your organisation to assess the difficulties you anticipate and prepare ways in which you propose to address them.

The people who will occupy the housing stock and the differences in their housing needs and desires are key considerations in developing a business plan. You should consider:

- age and age trends; both of current and future tenants
- ethnicity and race
- size of household
- type of household
- levels of employment
- trends in housing and welfare benefit dependence

A consideration of the profile of applicants, tenants and future tenants will provide a better understanding of what action is needed to meet their needs and therefore where and how resources should be prioritised.

This is what marketing text books call "segmenting the market" i.e. breaking the "market" or consumer base down into manageable pieces which can be assessed to determine their specific needs. Segmenting the consumer base will establish that there is a wide range of different needs in different 'client groups' which require different approaches.

The views of tenants and residents groups will provide a first hand source of information. Information can also be requested by conducting surveys, issuing questionnaires and speaking to callers at local offices and on home visits to ascertain their views about the service they receive and the difficulties they experience.

Physical factors may affect the way in which your organisation can develop. Some examples of the type of issue you may need to consider are:

- local geography: the ease with which your consumers and staff can travel
- the present nature of the locality in which you work:

- is it part of a regeneration programme
  e.g. City Challenge
- what are its specific design needs?
  Is there scope to make use of unused or under-used buildings?

Technological Environment

How will changes in technology alter the way you approach your function and deliver services?

What will be the impact of new communication systems and how well are you likely to be able to keep up with them?

Some assumptions will be required here but there is no doubt that developments in technology are continuing at a rapid pace. Many of the technological capabilities which currently exist which are taken for granted will become outdated. Nearly all housing practitioners will be able to cite difficulties associated with technological advancement therefore the need to pre-empt changes through the planning process is crucial.

External Analysis

Consider your results and prioritise action to address them based on:

- the scale of their impact if they do occur

- the probability of them happening

Do not spend excessive time on things which have a low probability of happening and will have little impact if they do happen.

Concern yourself primarily with those things which have a high probability of happening and which will have a substantial impact on your organisation if they happen.

3.4 Internal Analysis

The intention of analysing internal factors in a systematic way is to:

- place them in the context of the external environment
- consider those which are most likely to affect performance
- place the organisation in a position to realistically consider where it wants to be over the next 12 months and beyond
- consider the capability of the organisation to get to where it wants to be.

Culture

For the purpose of a business planning exercise, organisational culture can be defined as the "values and norms" of the organisation. The way people work together and what is and is not acceptable in the workplace.

If your organisation has a culture which is resistant to new ideas and new ways of working some preparatory work will be required before business planning can be introduced.

Is your organisation closer to the features described in the column headed 'mechanistic' or the one headed 'organic' in the table below?

Feature	Mechanistic	Organic
Individual	Separate	Related
Task Definition	Rigid	Fluid
Control	Vertical, based on rules	Loose and based on networks
Knowledge	Centralised	Anywhere and recognised to be anywhere
Communication	Vertical, Top–down	Horizontal and vertical in all directions
Commitment	To senior officer	To organisation and consumers

A mechanistic organisation is more resistant to change and therefore if your organisation veers this way it will be more difficult to instigate

Business Planning for Housing

business planning. It will also be difficult to use business planning as a tool which involves staff at all levels to achieve common ownership of organisational goals. For business planning to succeed, your organisation will need to move from *'mechanistic'* to *'organic'*. Some of the barriers associated with this form of organisation will need to be dismantled before business planning can be anything other than just a method of producing a document.

The following grid can be used as a starting point for cultural analysis:

Aspects of Culture		Some starting Questions
Beliefs & Values	1	What are the core beliefs of the organisation?
	2	How strongly are these held and in particular by whom?
	3	How pervasive are these beliefs at each level?
	4	Do they create strengths or weaknesses?
	5	Who are the role models or heroes?
Behaviour & Symbols	1	What behaviour is expected and rewarded (e.g. innovation, risk taking)?
	2	What language is used to describe the organisation (e.g. glamorous, derogatory)?
	3	What is the overriding attitude towards each stakeholder group?
Leadership & Style	1	Is the organisation mechanistic or organic?
	2	Which aspects of the organisation are stressed internally? externally? are they the same?
	3	Where is the power held? Is responsibility delegated? Does this match accountability?
	4	What attributes are sought in the recruitment and selection process? Are these different now from what they used to be?
Structure & Systems	1	Do the structures and systems encourage teamwork and collaboration or do they foster competition?
	2	What stress is placed on individual objectives at the expense of corporate objectives?
	3	Are structures and systems regularly reviewed and updated?
	4	What emphasis is placed on training and is it considered to be relevant to the needs of those who receive it?

Adapted from Scholes and Johnson

To achieve benefits from an exercise like this it may be necessary to take time away from the normal work environment. The use of an external and impartial facilitator will probably aid the process.

Examination of the culture of your housing association or local authority department provides an opportunity to understand better:

- what individuals think
- what sections or work groups think
- informal networks and inter-actions
- sources and bases of power within the organisation
- the existence of coalitions between individuals and groups
- conflicts of expectations and beliefs.

The extension of such an analysis to the external stakeholders of your organisation is recommended.

Personnel and Staffing

There are many issues related to personnel and staffing which should be considered as part of the business planning process. It is important to reiterate that you can only effect organisational change via the people who work for your organisation. Therefore if your business planning process indicates that substantial change is needed, this may require substantial change to your personnel and staffing practice.

Some of the issues to be aware of which may require attention are:

- work force planning
- recruitment and selection
- performance management and review
- remuneration and reward systems
- industrial relations procedures.

— How many staff does your organisation employ?

— How does this compare with 12 months ago 24 months ago etc.? Is there a trend?

— What is your grading structure? Is it appropriate?

— Do you have a way of planning and adjusting staffing levels in relation to variations in workload? for example, part time working, job sharing, fixed term and temporary contracts?

Business Planning for Housing

— Do your staff have appropriate levels of ability to address the challenges you have identified? for example;

— What proportion of your staff have housing or housing related qualifications?

— What level of financial training have line managers received?

— Have shortfalls been identified through a training needs analysis?

It will be necessary to reach opinions on whether the organisation has the right people to address the challenges it faces. If not, how can it be rectified?

Issue	Factors to Consider
The Right People	attitude capability commitment
The Right Rewards	market comparisons job sizing national / local bargaining trade union input

Organisation Structure

In addition to staff numbers and competencies you should assess the suitability of your organisation's structure. The design of your organisation should reflect the relationship between the tasks to be performed and the people who will perform them.

Unless you have recently undertaken a major restructure, it is likely that your structure will have been shaped by a number of small scale and ad hoc decisions. Most restructuring exercises involve small scale reallocation of duties between a small number of jobs. Business planning provides an opportunity to undertake a review of the interactions between different functional and geographical groups.

Is your structure providing the right number of staff and staff with appropriate skills where they are needed?

— Could your structure be top-heavy?

— Are senior staff spending too much time on clerical and administrative work?

— Is there scope for delegation of duties?

— If you have decentralised geographically have you devolved authority to the local level?

Flatter structures can improve service delivery and reduce staff costs but in themselves are not enough. The key to an appropriate organisation structure is to ensure that staff skills and abilities are aligned with workload.

Finance and Financial Systems

Finance is a focal part of the internal analysis. It underpins all that the organisation does. It will act as a constraining as well as an enabling factor. It is dealt with in more detail in Chapter Five.

Non-Staff Resources

In addition to staffing issues you will also need to consider non-staff resources available to your organisation such as:

- premises
- transport
- plant
- equipment

— Are they adequate?

— Are they in the right places?

— Do they meet the needs of staff and tenants and if not what is the effect of this?

— What are the shortcomings and how can they be rectified?

Many of the issues you consider under these headings may at first seem mundane. However it is often the mundane factors which have a significant impact on people. By drawing up a list of shortcomings you may be surprised at how many innovative ideas are generated and how many difficulties can be improved at minimal cost. For example, changing office layouts, reception areas, access to IT equipment.

Examining the Current Position — *Northern Counties Housing Association*

Northern Counties Housing Association (NCHA) commissioned external consultants to assist with its strategic review exercise. Part of the process consisted of eight workshop sessions, facilitated by the consultants, to take stock of the association's position.

This part of the process was attended by a team of eleven staff comprising the Chief Executive, all directors, two assistant directors and two line managers. The sessions were:

Session	Content
1	general introduction and objectives
2	identification of key external environmental factors
3	identification of key internal factors; identifying those which were strengths and those and those which were weaknesses; prioritisation of these and consideration of whether an objective or subjective analysis.
4 & 5	SWOT analysis undertaken bringing together the elements on internal strengths and weaknesses with external influences (opportunities and threats).
6	included the following work: — definition of where NCHA is — comment on the consultants' summary of where NCHA is — discussion of the business objectives which have got NCHA where it is — consideration of current activities and possible options for the future
7	finalisation of work on the SWOT analysis and discussion of the strategic options
8	review of the process

3.5 Summary

The strengths which your organisation has may be in any area of its work, activity or structure. It is important however to ensure that every one has the opportunity to contribute to this exercise of internal and external analysis.

The principle of brainstorming is that a problem is addressed by a group. Group members are allowed to let their imaginations run wild and no contribution should be scorned or rubbished. All contributions can be assessed at the end of the exercise. The overall objective of the approach described above is to create lists of strengths and weaknesses and opportunities and threats which have a substantial bearing on the purpose of the organisation.

Some examples of often quoted *strengths* are:

- committed work force
- good relationship with tenants
- strong level of reserves

And *weaknesses*:

- managers have little financial training
- housing stock requires substantial capital investment
- out–dated / deficient IT system.

There may be some issues which potentially fall into *both* categories:

- relatively low rent levels
- decentralised office structure
- generous pay for staff compared with local economy.

There may be strengths which seem so obvious that no one will dare say them for fear of stating the obvious. There is also a danger that weaknesses may be overlooked or staff will not be comfortable about speaking their mind about what they consider to be weaknesses. Both situations must be guarded against.

SWOT Analysis

Having considered the above factors your housing association or local authority will have a pretty good picture of itself and the world in which it is operating.

SWOT (**S**trengths, **W**eaknesses, **O**pportunities and **T**hreats) analysis is a method of summarising all the factors and setting an agenda for action.

The SWOT analysis is becoming well known within housing circles. Very often however, it never realises its full potential because:

- it represents only subjective views
- it is not linked to other aspects of the planning process i.e. it is done in isolation (SWOT analysis is not an end in itself)
- it is not channelled into priorities for action.

A number of organisations list their SWOT analysis in their business plan. In doing so, strengths and weaknesses are not pitched against opportunities and threats to consider their likely outcome. Without systematic analysis it is therefore difficult:

- to distil the relative magnitude of each factor
- to set a priority in which they should be addressed
- to determine an approach to addressing issues i.e. a strategy.

The strengths and weaknesses of the organisation will arise from the internal analysis and the threats and opportunities from the external analysis which has been conducted. At this stage these are perceptions or beliefs which have perhaps arisen from a brainstorming forum.

The analysis below is not technically accurate and like other similar approaches is not a stand-alone methodology which will provide conclusive results. It does however take your analysis to a point which will allow you to consider what your objectives should be a and how you might start to achieve them. It should be cross-referenced to other methodologies and will never eliminate subjectivity. Remember, such tools are decision support tools. But the decision cannot be made by the tool !

Chapter 3 • Taking Stock

Summary of SWOT Analysis
(Illustrative example)

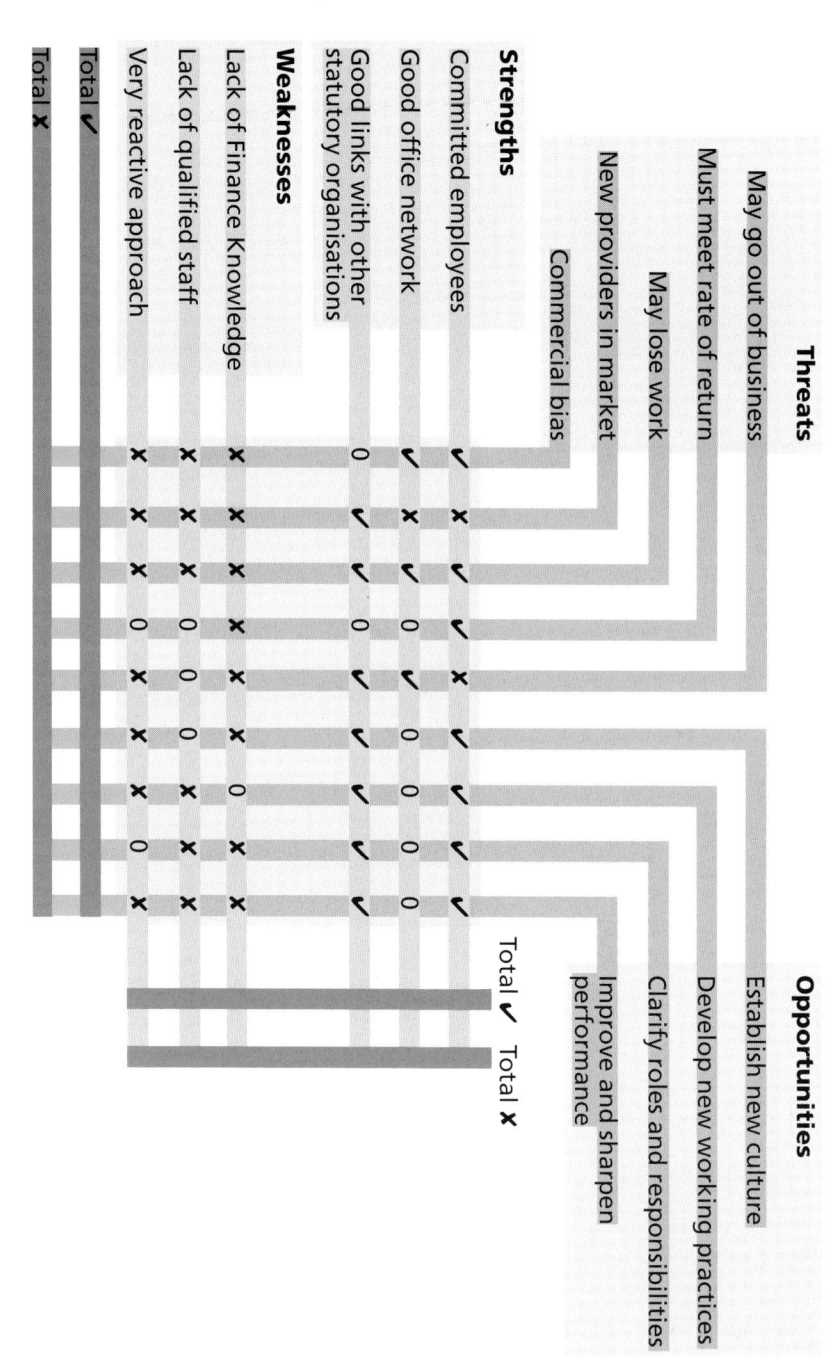

	Threats				**Opportunities**			
	May go out of business	Must meet rate of return	May lose work	New providers in market	Commercial bias	Establish new culture	Develop new working practices	Clarify roles and responsibilities	Improve and sharpen performance
Strengths									
Committed employees	✓	✓	0	x	x	✓	✓	✓	✓
Good office network	✓	x	x	✓	✓	✓	✓	✓	✓
Good links with other statutory organisations	0	✓	✓	✓	✓	✓	✓	✓	✓
Weaknesses									
Lack of Finance Knowledge									
Lack of qualified staff									
Very reactive approach									

Total ✓ Total x

Total ✓
Total x

45

Business Planning for Housing

Approach

1 Mark ✔ if there would be a benefit to the organisation, i.e. a strength would enable the organisation to take advantage of or counteract a problem arising from an environmental change.

2 Mark ✘ if there would be an adverse effect on the organisation i.e. a strength would be reduced by the environmental change or a weakness would prevent the organisation from overcoming the problems associated with the change or would be accentuated by that change.

3 Mark **0** if there will be no overall effect.

4 The completed article gives a clearer view of the extent to which the environmental changes and influences provide opportunities or threats given current resources and capabilities.

5 The resulting matrix can be used to prioritise action either in relation to environmental influences or strengths and weaknesses.

A SWOT analysis conducted in this way provides a device for systematically looking at strengths and weaknesses versus opportunities and threats and will give direction to your thoughts about objectives and strategies.

Chapter 4

Objectives and Strategies

This chapter:
- differentiates between objectives and strategies
- considers a structure for setting objectives and devising strategies.

By the end of this chapter the reader should:
- understand the difference between an objective and a strategy
- understand how objectives and strategies at different levels must inter-relate.

4.1 Introduction

This chapter is about addressing the parts of the business planning framework which ask; *"Where do we want to be?"* and *"How are we going to get there?"*

Organisations which have not clarified their objectives and strategies will have staff who do not understand their role in relation to other parts of their organisation. This will result in staff undertaking functions which are not central to the organisation's mission whilst other more important functions are not given sufficient priority.

An objective is a destination you seek to arrive at. A strategy is a way of travelling there.

For example, a housing association may establish that it has a poor level of tenant participation. To address this it sets itself a number of objectives, one of which is: "to increase the number of tenants' associations to achieve at least one association in each geographical area in which it owns properties by a set date."

It must then go on to develop a strategy to achieve this objective. It may decide to:

- appoint a tenant association development officer
- rekindle enthusiasm in tenants associations where it has dwindled
- establish new associations in areas where there is none.

By differentiating between objectives and strategies the association can be clear about:

- what it wants to achieve
- how it wants to achieve it.

The two issues must be made distinct in order that they can implemented and monitored effectively.

A business plan should show both objectives and strategies. By doing so the business plan becomes a working tool rather than a wish list. It sets out what needs to be done and how it will be done and thereby provides a documented reference point for monitoring both the implementation and the outcome. By stating objectives and stating how they will be implemented the business plan can map out the requirements in terms of staff and other resources.

Objectives and Strategies – *Charnwood Forest Housing Association*

Corporate objectives arise largely from the annual 'Back to the Future' weekend.

The association set as one its objectives, selection of new business areas to move into. The objective arose from the association's desire to reduce its reliance exclusively on Housing Corporation funded new build rental homes.

Chapter 4 • Objectives and Strategies

Agreed

Objectives should be agreed with the individual job holder to achieve ownership of the objective. This requires a two-way discussion between the line manager and the job holder to agree the measures of attainment required. Objectives should be agreed in a way that will promote individual development. This may mean that whilst the main focus should remain on achieving section or business unit objectives there may be personal objectives which are less focussed on these points but relate to development in a broader sense.

Realistic

The agreed objectives should be demanding but achievable. This requires that both the job holder and the line manager are realistic about the current position and do not set objectives which reflect a desirable but unattainable position. There should be a regular formal review and regular informal review and support from line managers.

Timed

All objectives should be set within an agreed time scale.

4.4　Selecting Strategies

Selecting strategies is about addressing the part of the business planning framework which asks; *"how are we going to get there?"*

Public service organisations have functions which they must undertake and roles which they would like to perform. The strategies which an organisation adopts will depend on the objectives it has decided upon. Even if your analysis confirms your current objectives you should still look at different ways of meeting those objectives.

Whatever objectives are selected there will undoubtedly be a variety of ways in which your housing department or housing association can set about achieving these.

Business Planning for Housing

Remember that a strategy is about how to do something. It must be translated into operational terms that relate to the procedures within your organisation.

It must be recognised that for most social housing organisations the strategic options available are limited. There is no assertion here that the choices available to a local authority or housing association are as wide as those in the private sector. Nevertheless clarifying strategies and procedures will help to increase efficiency and effectiveness by refining procedures and inter-dependencies.

Selecting Strategies

What must we do?
- statutory and policy requirements
- contract requirements

What must we not do?
- legal and policy restraints

What can we do?
- options
- building on strengths and opportunities
- minimising weaknesses and threats

Strategy Evaluation

It will be impossible to develop strategies for all objectives which satisfy all stakeholders

The process of setting objectives and developing strategies to meet those objectives needs to take account of the corporate circumstances and polices of the organisation. Setting the objectives and developing strategies must remain within the parameters of what the organisation is and is not prepared to do (see glossary at Chapter Two).

Strategies should be evaluated in relation to their:

- acceptability
- feasibility
- suitability

Chapter 4 • Objectives and Strategies

- cultural fit.

Acceptability

The acceptability of an organisation's strategies will need to be assessed in a variety of ways.

Even if objectives are well meaning the route to meeting those objectives must also be suitable for the organisation. This raises the issue of governance. In a local authority, elected members should provide the checks and balances and in a housing association it should be the committee members. In addition to this use should be made of other representative committees or forums.

An objective of rent arrears reduction by a certain amount by a certain date is a suitable and specific objective with which few people would take issue. The acceptability of the strategy to be adopted in meeting that objective is not necessarily the same in all organisations.

The organisation will need to address its stance on for example:

- advice, assistance and counselling
- distraint
- eviction

In many cases it will be possible to evaluate strategies in relation to existing policies. Where new proposals for ways of doing things are under consideration managers may need to secure agreement from elected or voluntary members.

Feasibility

The feasibility of a strategy to meet an objective is concerned with the question "can the strategy be implemented "?

In a public service environment feasibility usually comes down to resource allocation and the trade off between achieving one objective at the expense of another.

At its most basic level the issue of feasibility comes down to the question:

> *"can it (the strategy to meet the objective) be funded?"*

To answer this question effectively you may need to take financial advice. Ideally a robust methodology for costing proposals is required.

If the answer to this question is "yes" questions must be asked about whether the capability exists to implement it. This may be in terms of human or physical resources.

On issues of management systems the subject of feasibility may revolve around the capability of information technology.

Feasibility in terms of time scale must also be considered.

Suitability
The suitability of strategies must be linked with the findings of the environmental analysis. An important measure of evaluation is the degree to which any strategy is linked to the situation described in the environmental analysis.

Consideration of a strategy must have regard for the policies of the organisation.

Strategies should be assessed in relation to how far they go towards overcoming the weaknesses the organisation has recognised it has and maximising the strengths it considers it has:

- what effect is decentralisation likely to have in an organisation with poor communication?
- are staff with a strong training base being used appropriately?

Cultural Fit
The selection of strategies is inherently linked with the culture of an organisation. There is likely to be a pre-disposition to select strategies which fit the culture but it may not always be possible to select strategies which are fully in tune with the existing culture of the organisation. If this is the case you will need to address how far you can go in implementing that strategy.

4.5 Setting Objectives and Strategies – The Process

As with any cyclical process, it is difficult to know where to begin. The usual dilemma in setting objectives and developing strategies to meet them is whether to begin at the top or the bottom.

Top Down
- may be quicker
- may provide a strong and positive lead

Chapter 4 • Objectives and Strategies

- may lead to criticisms of autocratic management
- may miss the opportunity to achieve full involvement

Bottom Up
- may take a long time
- may improve morale and feelings of staff value
- may provide information not known to senior staff
- may lead to compromises
- may loose sight of corporate objectives

Planning Care Services — *East Dorset Housing Association*

Following stock transfer and the creation of East Dorset Housing Association (EDHA) analysis of its environment established that the Association's stance in respect of Community Care was an issue which EDHA must address. EDHA's first corporate plan produced in March 1994 stated its strategic objective to achieve a clear view of the Association's role in Community Care. The method by which this was to be achieved was by undertaking a comprehensive review of Care Services. Guidelines and terms of reference were agreed to project manage the review, together with the important step of nominating a senior manager within the Association to act as project manager. A timescale of 18 months was set.

Through regular team meetings, the wardens and control centre operators clearly defined current services and highlighted the issues which needed to be addressed. This was documented in a 'position' statement. The position statement was developed further by small groups analysing the care services in the form of a SWOT analysis for each service area in which EDHA operates. The analysis was followed by discussion about how the Association should or could respond to the issues arising from the analysis. This was developed into a detailed plan.

The review was reported to the Housing Services Sub-Committee on a regular basis as it progressed. A monitoring process was thereby sustained as the project developed.

A quality team was set up whose function it was to implement the plan which had been established by the larger group. The quality project team was comprised of key Officers in different areas of the delivery of care services. A project plan was produced based on the prioritised objectives set by the larger group. However, it became the responsibility of the quality team to implement the plan. This was done by producing a series of action sheets which detailed involvement from a wider group of staff.

The project and the action taken ensured a thorough review of Care Services at EDHA and objectives set were incorporated within the Association's 1995/96 Business Plan.

A compromise which can be used is to set corporate objectives and strategies and use this as a starting point for the involvement of staff. This means that staff have something to respond to which is often better than starting with a blank sheet of paper.

Introducing Business Planning — *Warwick District Council*

Business planning was introduced in the Housing Department as part of a corporate business planning initiative. Chief Officers were requested to identify 'business units' within their departments and each business unit produced its own business plan.

It was accepted that the first round of business planning for the 1994/95 period would be a first stab which would require further refinement in subsequent years. The first year of business planning was also viewed as a learning exercise which would assist business unit managers to get to grips with issues such as performance indicators, pricing and costing, budgetary planning and control etc.

The instigation of business planning within the housing department at Warwick has enabled staff at all levels to establish their purpose and their roles. It will lead to refinement of departmental objectives and performance indicators and will assist in the process of identifying unit costs.

The housing department at Warwick adopted a top down and a bottom up approach to business planning. The Chief Housing Officer developed specific objectives from the existing Strategy for Housing, whilst the various section heads and teams within the department considered the processes which would enable them to meet those objectives for which they are responsible.

Chapter 4 • Objectives and Strategies

There are organisations which have prided themselves on delegated management and devolved responsibility which have later found that their objectives lack corporacy and in some cases directly conflict with each other. Conversely there are organisations which have missed the opportunity to gain valuable insights from their own staff because they have taken a centralist approach.

Experience in organisations which have already developed business planning shows that addressing the business planning cycle from any extreme is likely to result in difficulties which have to be rectified later.

Gaining Commitment — *Lewisham LBC*

Clear communication of the departmental Business Plan to all staff has been vital element in ensuring its effective implementation. The Plan is initially presented to staff by the Director of Housing at the annual staff conference.

Workshop style sessions are then convened with every Service Unit by a member of the Departmental Management Team. In 1995 the event was titled "Thrive in '95" and involved each team working together to agree personal and collective contributions to the Business Plan objectives. These proposals were then presented by each team to the rest of the Service Unit. This approach has proved to be a potent tool to engender commitment by encouraging staff to focus on their contribution to each objective.

4.6 Structure of Strategies

You should aim to achieve a hierarchy of strategies which mirrors your hierarchy of objectives. In devising your strategies you should test that they are compatible with the strategies which will be undertaken at the tier above and below.

Strategies need to be translated into individual action plans. These are the steps which sequentially move individuals towards their objectives and thereby move the section, the business unit and eventually the entire organisation towards its objectives. This can be done once objectives have been agreed between job holders and line managers.

Business Planning for Housing

Action plans should:

- who is responsible for each activity
- who will monitor progress and performance
- how performance will be reviewed.

Action plans can be used retrospectively as well as prospectively. They provide a starting point for analysing reasons why objectives have not been met or if they have been met, how the time scale in meeting them in the future could be improved.

Timing

The question of when to commence the planning cycle also has no simple answer. Ideally it will be tied to the budget cycle but in practice this is difficult. Starting the planning process before the budget is known is likely to result in revision to the plan. Starting after will provide no chance of setting individual targets before the time they are due to commence.

In subsequent years the timing of the process will become less difficult. Many decisions to be made will be based on priorities which have been previously decided. Updates and revision should in any case be an on-going process.

Chapter 5

Finance

This chapter:
- explains the financial statements which should be included in a business plan
- considers the use of budgets and cost accounting.

By the end of this chapter the reader should:
- be aware of the main types of financial information which would normally be included in a business plan
- understand the difference between financial accounting and management accounting
- be aware of the importance of cost accounting as a tool to evaluate objectives and strategies.

5.1 Introduction

This chapter is not intended to be a free-standing financial text. To be effective, plans must backed by financial information. This chapter considers financial planning as the corollary of service planning.

All decisions about service delivery have financial implications. Most decisions about changes in service delivery have financial implications.

Business Planning for Housing

Accounting information is required within organisations in order to enable the organisation to understand the financial consequences of changing external or internal circumstances. Financial management is an art, not an exact science. Its application depends on the person or people interpreting a variety of accounting principles. It should be viewed as a support service within your organisation. Accounting control systems cannot be developed in isolation and indeed should not lead the organisation.

This chapter is intended to increase awareness and understanding of the financial elements of the business planning process. It is not intended to instruct the reader how to compile financial statements and apply accounting practise.

Financial Planning — *English Churches Housing Group*

In English Churches Housing Group's (ECHG) first business plan, financial models were prepared by a consultant. Whilst the result was satisfactory, the model produced was not owned by the organisation.

ECHG has now developed its own business planning financial models which are improved and enhanced annually.

The financial models reflect the organisation's operations and have sufficient information to provide an overall picture of the business. The parameters used in the modelling are capable of being stressed in different ways in order to test a wide range of different scenarios and their likely out turns.

Within the business plan there is a wide range of financial targets which the association expects to achieve and the annual budget is assessed against these. There is a quarterly review, both on performance against budget and against other parts of the business plan to ensure that ECHG is meeting its overall objectives.

This process has been extremely useful to ECHG in identifying where the particular pressure points are likely to be in the future and the main risk factors. The association is much clearer about the financial parameters within which it is working and the returns it expects to achieve.

5.2 Financial Accounting and Management Accounting

Accounting has its origin in the role of stewardship. In addition to this its present purpose is to aid decision making, planning and control. Financial accounting information is largely for external users whereas management accounting information is for use within the organisation.

Financial Accounting

Financial accounting has its emphasis on past events and the organisation's external relationships. It must meet the statutory requirements set down for local authorities and housing associations. It has three key facets:

i) internal control; to ensure the regular collection and payment of monies due and to prevent and detect inefficiency and dishonesty in this process.

ii) measurement of financial information; to provide proper and accurate records of the financial transactions which are required of the organisation.

iii) reporting; to report the financial position to investors and other stakeholders, usually through the production of annual accounts.

Management Accounting

Financial accounts are not on their own sufficient to meet the needs of decision makers. To enable an organisation to survive, plans have to be translated into financial costs and benefits. This is the realm of management accounting.

Management accounting is part of the process of organisational control. Management accounting information therefore needs to be used in conjunction with more informal and qualitative information which is available to those who will make decisions about the organisation. Accounting information is used in the commercial sector to provide indicators of overall performance for example:

- return on capital employed
- return on investment.

Its role in public sector organisations has traditionally been more for budgetary control. The changing framework of social housing requires a more highly developed form of management accounting information.

5.3 Main Financial Statements

The three main financial statements usually contained in a business plan are the:

- balance sheet

- income and expenditure account

- cashflow forecast.

These statements are produced at least annually and are usually included in an organisation's annual report. Because planning is about looking forward, these statements need to be projected forward to show that business plans are financially viable. The projection is usually over a three or five year period.

Financial Planning — *Devon & Cornwall Housing Association*

The objective of the financial models used in the association's business planning process is to provide a computer model which allows the impact of changes in the financial environment to be seen instantly.

The first step in building the models was to identify the financial impact that would arise from possible decisions made within the association. For example: rent setting policies, level of housing stock due to be added, borrowing strategies. The association also had to identify the variables which are outside its control but which also would affect its financial position. For example, interest rates and inflation. Having identified both sets of variables, the computer model was used to develop an 'Input Section' which can be used to see the result of different permutations of the financial variables.

Consultation with all departments was essential to eliminate errors and omissions in translating service plans into financial plans. The model was extensively reviewed and tested to ensure that it worked correctly.

Chapter 5 • Finance

> The computer model feeds through to a number of calculation workbooks which in turn feed through to a report section which consists of an Income and Expenditure Statement, a Balance Sheet and a Cashflow Statement for each financial year for which the association is planning.

Balance Sheet

The balance sheet is a snapshot of an organisation's position at a given point in time, usually the year end. It does not show activity over a time period.

It shows on one side, the assets which the organisation has (the uses to which resources have been put) and on the other side, how those assets have been financed (where the resources have come from). Both sides of the statement must be equal i.e. must balance.

Within the balance sheet, the assets of the organisation can be divided into those which are fixed and those which are current.

Fixed assets are those resources which are retained over several accounting periods i.e. several years. They are used to enable the organisation to fulfil its function. Most obviously in our case this is the housing stock.

Current assets are those of a more immediate nature, although they may sometimes stretch over more than a single financial year.

The other side of the balance sheet contains details of the capital and reserves which are used to fund the assets *(See example over)*.

Social Housing Association Balance Sheet

	1994/95 £ 000's	1995/96 £ 000's	1996/97 £ 000's
Fixed Assets			
Housing Properties at Cost	26592	30580	35670
Less Housing Association Grant	-18768	-21371	-24308
Other Fixed Assets	176	198	215
Current Assets			
Investments	1112	2061	2848
Cash	985	895	834
Debtors	134	114	103
Current Liabilities			
Creditors falling due within 1 year	263	296	318
Net Current Assets	1968	2774	3467
Total Assets Less Current Liabilities	**9792**	**12181**	**15044**
Long Term Loans	5824	7365	9453
Capital and Reserves			
Accumulated Surplus	2915	3405	3971
Designated Reserves	1053	1411	1620
	9792	**12181**	**15044**

NB Creditors are people to whom the organisation owes money and are treated as a liability for accounting purposes. Debtors are people who owe money to the organisation and are treated as an asset for accounting purposes.

The business plan may have considered issues such as the acquisition of properties and the loans which will be required to achieve this. Projecting such decisions over the period of the business plan and translating these into financial sums will provide a picture of the organisation's situation at the end of each financial year.

This will ensure that the figures stack up and will provide a profile of the changing nature of the organisation over the period of the plan.

Income and Expenditure Account

The title of this account is self-explanatory. The usual accounting period is the financial year although some housing associations use a calendar year. This account may well be prepared on a more regular basis. This statement collects together revenue items of income and expenditure.

As with the balance sheet, the income and expenditure account is projected forward across the period of the business plan in relation to the likely changes to income and expenditure as a consequence of the proposed amendments to service delivery and other ongoing commitments *(See example over)*.

Cash Flow Forecast

The cash flow forecast summarises the cash inflows and outflows for the organisation for the period of the business plan. This is an important financial statement because it is not sufficient solely for an organisation to remain "out of the red". Many organisations fail to survive not because they are not profitable, but because of lack of liquid assets i.e. they do not have funds available when they are needed. The planning process must take care to ensure that funds are available in order to meet regular commitments e.g. loan repayments, salaries etc.

The business plan will usually show cashflow year on year but for this to be managed effectively the annual figures will need to be supported by a monthly cash flow forecast.

Collecting the figures to put in the forecast statement is difficult to do accurately. By devising a forecast of what the position should be during each year of the business plan provides a better opportunity to take action if things start to go wrong *(See example over)*.

Social Housing Asociation
Income And Expenditure Account

	1994/95 £ 000's	1995/96 £ 000's	1996/97 £ 000's
Income			
Rent	2980	3248	3702
Service Charges	264	276	289
	3244	**3524**	**3991**
Expenditure			
Housing Management	259	284	325
Mortgage Payments	542	638	763
Property Depreciation	148	192	235
Cyclical Repairs	203	214	226
Responsive Repairs	213	231	243
Service and Hostel Charges	1144	1245	1421
Major Repairs Provision	358	379	388
	2867	**3183**	**3601**
Surplus	377	341	390
Investment Income	134	142	167
Other Income	6	7	9
Net Surplus	**517**	**490**	**566**
Accumulated Surplus *Brought Forward*	2607	2915	3405
Accumulated Surplus *Carried Forward*	**2915**	**3405**	**3971**

Social Housing Association
Cash Flow Forecast

	1994/95 £000's	1995/96 £000's	1996/97 £000's
Revenue Income			
Rent and Service Charges	3244	3524	3991
Investment Income	134	142	167
Other Income	25	22	24
	3403	**3688**	**4182**
Revenue Expenditure			
Housing Management	259	284	325
Loan Repayments	542	638	763
Cyclical Repairs	203	214	226
Responsive Repairs	213	231	243
Service and Hostel Charges	1144	1245	1421
Planned Maintenance	328	337	364
Other Expenditure	53	34	35
	2742	**2983**	**3377**
Revenue Surplus/(Deficit)	**661**	**705**	**805**
Capital Receipts			
Housing Association Grant	1105	2325	2145
Sales Receipts	397	65	115
Transfer from Loan Accounts	524	1965	2365
	2026	**4355**	**4625**
Capital Expenditure			
Housing	2457	4123	3924
Transfer to Loan Accounts	174	32	210
	2631	**4155**	**4134**
Capital Surplus/(Deficit)	**(605)**	**200**	**491**
Total Surplus/(Deficit)	**56**	**905**	**1296**
Cash Balance *Brought Forward*	2218	2274	3179
Cash Balance *Carried Forward*	2274	3179	4475

Business Planning for Housing

Most housing association business plans already include the statements discussed above. Housing association accounts are now required to conform with the format of accounts for PLCs (public limited companies). The situation for local authorities in the post CCT period will resemble this more closely.

The situation for housing management contractors after CCT will largely conform with the position described above in respect of the cash flow forecast and the income and expenditure account. Where the Council's DSO is successful, there will be a DSO revenue account. This is the DSO's income and expenditure account. This will be supported by one or more 'Trading Accounts'. An example of a trading account is shown below.

Trading Account

Expenditure	£ million	Income	£ million
Employees	2.2	Charge to Client	4.9
Running Costs	0.8		
Capital Charges	0.3		
Support Service Costs	1.4		
Budgeted Surplus	0.2		
Total	**4.9**		**4.9**

The planning process for the client side of the local authority structure will also need to include financial projections. This part of the Housing Revenue Account (the client account) will include those costs associated with the policy, enabling and monitoring function of the housing service. It will also include those costs relating to parts of the housing service which have not been tendered.

5.4 Cost Accounting

Compiling the statements described above requires knowledge of the costs of providing services.

In a competitive environment with separate client and contractor organisations it is not possible to adjust rents to meet increased expenditure and subsidy is not available to bridge deficits. It is imperative that local authorities and housing associations maintain tight control of their costs. In order to do this they must first be able to identify the components of their overall costs.

Budgets are made up from adding together the money available to undertake a number of different activities. The overall budget is the sum total of the money available to the organisation or department. Organisations should be able to group their costs by function and by geographical area in the case of decentralised service provision.

A cost centre is a logical grouping of budgets relating to either:

- a function which is undertaken at a number of places, or
- a number of different functions undertaken at a certain place e.g. an area housing office.

The budget can be broken down into a number of different sub totals, often called budget heads. As each of the budget heads applies to a different type of function e.g. amount available for management of repairs, amount available for supplies and stationery we can call these functional cost centres.

In a housing service operating from more than one geographical location it may be considered appropriate to delegate the budget for each of the functions undertaken to the local offices from where the housing service is provided. The budgets for the functions undertaken at the local office can then be grouped together to form a geographical cost centre.

The starting point for an analysis of current budgets is to group all the activities undertaken by the association or housing department by function and also to group those functions according to the locality at which they are delivered. This can be done by developing a budget matrix. An example for a local authority DSO which is operating in a post CCT setting having won all four of the local authority's housing management contracts is shown below.

Business Planning for Housing

Borough Council

Preparation for Housing Management CCT

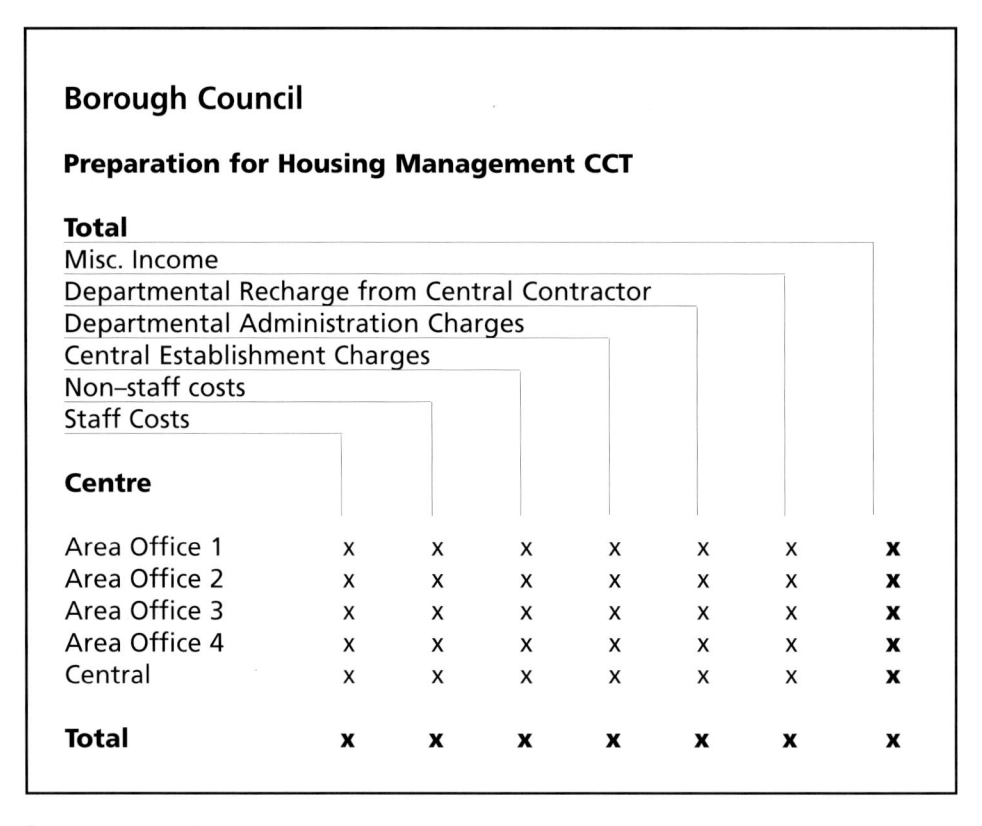

Total
Misc. Income
Departmental Recharge from Central Contractor
Departmental Administration Charges
Central Establishment Charges
Non–staff costs
Staff Costs

Centre

Area Office 1	x	x	x	x	x	x	x
Area Office 2	x	x	x	x	x	x	x
Area Office 3	x	x	x	x	x	x	x
Area Office 4	x	x	x	x	x	x	x
Central	x	x	x	x	x	x	x
Total	**x**	**x**	**x**	**x**	**x**	**x**	**x**

figure 5.1 Cost Centre Matrix

In theory it is possible to build up a budget matrix like this from scratch. This is known as a zero based budget. In practice however this is unlikely to happen because many of the costs which you incur will be pre-determined. For example if you have an existing complement of staff which does not have the grade or skill mix which you would like, this cannot be changed instantly. In the same way, many non staff costs cannot be altered other than in the long term.

Costing is an important part of business planning because setting objectives and determining strategies have costs associated with them. There is clearly little point in setting strategies to meet objectives if those strategies cannot be resourced. Being able to cost services properly provides a powerful source of information to inform your planning process.

5.5 Summary

The financial contribution to the business planning process should be made by accountants. It is not therefore necessary for housing managers to be able to draw up the financial statements considered above. It is however necessary to understand the relationship between service planning and financial planning.

A thorough consideration of budgetary control is provided in 'Managing Housing Budgets in a Competitive Environment" by David Garland and John Parker (Longman/CIH 1993).

Chapter 6

Performance Review and Staff Appraisal

This chapter:
- emphasises that business planning is an cyclical process and must involve those who are responsible for turning plans into reality
- asserts that this can be achieved by a structured framework of performance management as part of the business planning cycle.

By the end of this chapter the reader should:
- understand performance review as a part of the business planning cycle.

6.1 Introduction

This chapter is about addressing that part of the business planning framework which asks; "How do we know whether we are getting there?" Monitoring performance is the link which completes the business planning cycle.

Review is required not just at a corporate level but for all the sub units/ cost centres/ local offices for which objectives were set. It is required for

Chapter 6 • Performance Review and Staff Appraisal

all individuals within those sub units; indeed for all staff within the organisation.

Performance review may be viewed as the last link if we are considering an organisation which is engaging in the business planning process for the first time. In subsequent years the 'review' process will actually inform the stages which were considered in earlier chapters. The process, as a circle, has no beginning and no end.

6.2 Performance Review

Performance review is part of the wider concept of performance management. Business planning itself is an approach to performance management. Performance review relies on effective monitoring of results. The creation of action plans, discussed in Chapter Four, which establish clear responsibilities provides a starting point for performance review.

Many organisations have operated some kind of personal performance review or performance appraisal system for a considerable time. There is nothing profoundly different about the nature of performance appraisal as part of business planning. But as part of the business planning process it must be strongly linked with the objectives and strategies which your housing association or housing department has decided to adopt.

The review process should:

- be co-ordinated with review of the organisational tiers above and below it
- be part of a timetabled approach throughout the year
- be aligned with any other organisational initiatives e.g. "Investors in People", vocational training qualifications
- provide a method of feedback so that there is information to senior managers who are responsible for strategic decision-making.

6.3 Structure

In chapter four we considered the need for a hierarchy of objectives. The objectives which are set at all levels in the hierarchy need to be reviewed. Thus, the review process can be seen as

Business Planning for Housing

- individual / personal.
- business unit / section
- directorate / department
- corporate

In effect an inverted form of the same hierarchy.

A good performance review system must have:

- objective measures of performance
- a system to assess performance against the measures
- a feed forward device to inform the planning process.

Business planning is about achieving co-ordination throughout the service which is being provided. If objectives fit well with the tier above and below so the review process should do the same.

Therefore the summation of individual reviews informs review of the business unit, summation of business unit reviews informs directorate/departmental review and so on. Corporate review therefore is not a mystical performance measure but a solidly founded assessment of the degree to which all the component parts of the organisation have achieved their stated objectives.

There is however a danger that the review process at different levels is not co-ordinated. Corporate performance review and personal performance review are used increasingly but integration is difficult. Some pitfalls are likely to be:

- mis-matching of objectives at different levels
- review process is absent at middle tiers
- objectives which are only achievable at the expense of other parts of the organisation.

Indicators of performance are important in order to develop objective assessment of strengths and weaknesses in the level of performance within various parts of the organisation.

6.4 Effectiveness

Making your performance review process an effective one requires that every aspect of activity for which objectives are set should have a named manager or supervisor who is accountable for meeting agreed objectives.

Chapter 6 • Performance Review and Staff Appraisal

The best designed performance review system will serve little purpose if it is not taken seriously. There is still resistance to formal performance review in a number of housing organisations.

First, your organisation must grasp the nettle and undertake to formalise its performance review process if this is not already the case. Secondly, the links between objectives and strategies at all levels must be made clear within the organisation. Finally, sensitive and awkward issues must not be avoided because ignoring weaknesses will prevent the review process from informing the next round of objective setting.

To be effective your organisation's performance review process must be viewed within a culture of critical appraisal. Whilst recognising effort and attainment this will encourage staff at all levels to look for opportunities to improve the services they provide.

Performance Review — *Charnwood Forest Housing Association*

Performance appraisal is an integral part of the business planning cycle. (See diagram in chapter 2). All staff, on a team basis, are involved in setting their own team's objectives for the forthcoming year. These are developed from the corporate objectives arising from the annual 'Back to the Future' weekend.

There are Personal Development Reviews for all staff at which some time is spent looking back at past achievements and areas where there is scope for improvement. Each line manager has at least two individual sessions with his/her staff ; one where they agree core and development objectives and training needs, one where they review progress.

Personal Development Reviews consider individual objectives in relation to the team objectives which have been set. The meeting seeks to establish agreement between line manager and staff member, about the core development objectives for that individual and in so doing, it establishes training needs. This ensures that each staff member knows their own core and development objectives and that appropriate training and support is identified to enable the member of staff to achieve the objectives. This meeting sets the scene for the review meeting.

6.5   Individual Appraisal

Personal appraisal is necessary to set and review objectives and to ensure that there is proper linkage between personal objectives and the wider section objectives and service objectives.

Personal appraisal should be concerned to:

- increase the satisfaction of staff with their organisation
- increase the satisfaction of the organisation with its staff.

To do this the appraisal system must:

- identify the employee's training and development needs and set in train the means by which they can be satisfied
- assist each employee to meet the standard of performance required of him/her in order to achieve personal objectives and contribute to business unit objectives.

Both aspects of the appraisal must be approached in a way that fits within the hierarchy of objectives.

Training is one way of assisting members of staff to meet their required standard of performance. This can be addressed at the appraisal discussion. But not all the development steps which lead to increased performance can be addressed through a training course. The appraisal discussion must therefore be clear both in setting out the objectives and in determining the degree to which previous objectives were achieved. For those which were not achieved either fully or partially, the appraisee and the appraiser should reach agreement on what needs to be done to rectify the situation.

The Review Process — *Lewisham LBC*

Review of individual performance is linked to the business planning process through the appraisal system. In Lewisham this takes the form of an Employee Development Scheme (EDS) and a Development Needs Analysis (DNA) interview. EDS is concerned with agreeing individual performance targets; DNA focusses on each employee producing a personal development plan.

These interviews then build up a training needs analysis on a team, Service Unit and organisation–wide level. These can be reviewed in line with the department's service needs and used to influence the content

Chapter 6 • Performance Review and Staff Appraisal

of the following year's business plan. The key to success has been ensuring that every one is skilled, competent and motivated to achieve their role successfully to achieve team, Service Unit and departmental objectives (see illustration below).

Members and customers play a part in the review process and quarterly progress reports are considered by Housing Committee.

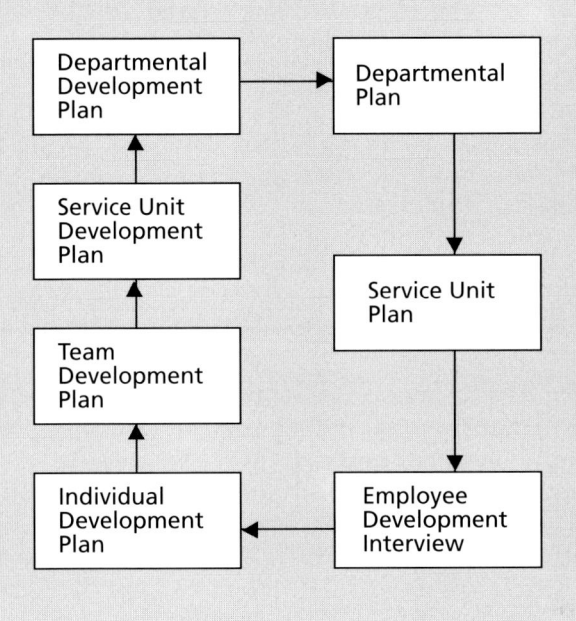

```
┌──────────────┐      ┌──────────────┐
│ Departmental │─────▶│ Departmental │
│ Development  │      │ Plan         │
│ Plan         │      └──────┬───────┘
└──────▲───────┘             │
       │                     │
┌──────┴───────┐             │
│ Service Unit │             ▼
│ Development  │      ┌──────────────┐
│ Plan         │      │ Service Unit │
└──────▲───────┘      │ Plan         │
       │              └──────┬───────┘
┌──────┴───────┐             │
│ Team         │             │
│ Development  │             │
│ Plan         │             ▼
└──────▲───────┘      ┌──────────────┐
       │              │ Employee     │
┌──────┴───────┐      │ Development  │
│ Individual   │◀─────│ Interview    │
│ Development  │      └──────────────┘
│ Plan         │
└──────────────┘
```

In its report on performance management (1995), the Audit Commission stated that staff must:

- understand what is required of them
- be trained in how to perform their role
- be committed to achieving what is required of them.

Personal appraisal is usually carried out on a one to one discussion basis. The annual or bi-annual discussion should consider past and current performance in relation to existing objectives and should revise future personal objectives within the context of the changes to business unit and corporate objectives.

Because performance review will inform the next cycle of business planning it is important that the appraisal interview is not treated as a one way process. If objectives which were set previously were not achieved because they were in appropriate or did not take account of changing circumstances there should be an opportunity for this to be discussed and addressed in order that it is not repeated.

6.6 Performance Indicators

Only time will tell whether the organisation actually got to where it wanted. However, it is not satisfactory to wait until the end of the year and then consider whether objectives were achieved. Information about whether the organisation is on course and on schedule to meet the objectives which were set is required. The information required to make decisions about whether the organisation is on course and on schedule provides the most relevant indicators of performance.

Review and monitoring must be part of an on-going process. Objectives are not written in tablets of stone, even when they have been written in your business plan, and therefore can be altered in the light of changing priorities and circumstances throughout the year. Do not be afraid to alter objectives and priorities. Developing a business planning process which will allow you to do so is the only way your business plan can be a working document rather than a glossy brochure.

Having set objectives the you need to ask:

- what information do we need to be able to monitor the progress we are making towards our objectives?
- to whom should the data be reported?
- how frequently?

The most important criteria for any performance indicator is that it should be appropriate to the objective on which it is designed to provide an indication of performance. Therefore the indicators which an organisation deems to be most appropriate will depend on the objectives which it has set and the strategies it has determined to meet those objectives. Because there will be objectives at each level in the organisation there will need to be performance indicators at each level.

Some examples of performance indicators are:

Corporate
Objective: To increase stock size by 5 % by year-end (in line with agreed time scale)

Indicator: Number of handovers (reported to committee monthly)

Chapter 6 • Performance Review and Staff Appraisal

Section Objective: To process all invoices within seven days of receipt

Indicator: Percentage of invoices processed within seven days

Individual Objective: Prepare all invoices received for verification within 24 hours or less

Indicator: Percentage of invoices received for verification within 24 hours of receipt

Performance indicators at different levels, their type and purpose are illustrated in the diagram below.

Data for	Purpose of Data	Type of Data	Frequency of Data
Top Management / members / the public	To review overall performance	Key indicators	Annual
Middle Managers	Monitor, intervene if necessary	Summarised data e.g. summarised arrears levels	Monthly or quarterly operating statements
Front line managers and staff	Take immediate action	Raw data e.g. arrears of individual tenants	Weekly or even daily

The publication of external performance indicators both by the Audit Commission and the Housing Corporation relate to corporate performance. The indicators provide inter-authority or inter-association comparisons. Such published indicators should not detract attention from the indicators of performance which are required within an organisation as part of the process of performance management. It was stated earlier and it is worth repeating that corporate development can only be effected through individual development.

6.7 Links with other Issues

There are a variety of personal and organisational development initiatives which local authority housing departments and housing associations are involved with. Some examples are:

- Investors in People
- National Vocational Qualifications or Scottish Vocational Qualifications
- BS 5750 / ISO 9000
- secondments / exchanges
- training

Links with Other Issues: Training – *Lewisham LBC*

Business Planning has been used to co-ordinate a plethora of performance, quality and service development issues. It has been used to ensure that what staff are skilled, competent and motivated to do corresponds to what Lewisham Housing needs them to do.

In 1994 Lewisham became the first large housing organisation in the country to achieve the 'Investors in People' award. The initiative provided a useful framework to test the effectiveness of the business planning process. Part of the assessment for IIP involved over 100 randomly selected staff being questioned by assessors about their understanding of the Business Plan, their contribution to it and how senior management had communicated this. Similarly, the Plan has been an essential element in the contract review work which Lewisham has undertaken for its repairs and caretaking services to attain accreditation to ISO 9002 (BS 5750).

The organisation has developed a sharp focus on producing training and development programmes to ensure that it can evaluate the return it receives in terms of achieving its business plan objectives. All training is now tested to ensure that all participants achieve an acceptable level of competence and all programmes are evaluated at individual, team and organisation-wide level in terms of their contribution to improving the implementation of strategies.

Chapter 6 • Performance Review and Staff Appraisal

Training Example – Rent Arrears

Every member of staff dealing with rent arrears, from Director to front line, has had to attend a three day course and sit a test to demonstrate competence. Those failing the competence test were required to attend elements of the course again until an acceptable level of competence was achieved. This programme, coupled with other initiatives has enabled the housing department to reduce rent arrears by £2.5 million in two years.

Training Example – Business Management

Lewisham Housing set up an innovative Post-Graduate Certificate in Management programme accredited by Thames Valley University in 1994. The programme has been designed to meet the specific business needs of Lewisham Housing and enable fulfilment of assignment to be achieved in the workplace. One module is devoted to business planning processes and techniques and managers have been able to develop their business plans both to fulfil their managerial responsibilities and to gain a qualification.

....

Development issues such as these should have been considered as part of the objective setting and strategy setting process described in Chapter Four. They should therefore be built into both performance review and management development and clearly must also be linked with budget setting.

For example, Investors in People and National Vocational Qualifications will have targets which can be used as performance review targets at an individual level. BS 5750 / ISO 9000 can be incorporated into the review and development of financial and management systems such as the internal control systems for newly established cost centres. Secondments and professional training can be used as part of individual and organisational development.

There are many other initiatives such as these which may be going on at any time. But because there are so many and often diverse initiatives it is crucial that they are focused. Introducing initiatives such as those listed above without asking what the organisation will obtain from them will not result in the best use of those resources. Business planning provides a method of establishing that focus.

6.8 Summary

As with other elements of business planning, performance review should be treated as a continuous process. A timetable or schedule may be required but be aware that it may be necessary to deviate from this on occasions. As has been suggested earlier, events do not always accord with the plans which were made.

Performance review and and staff appraisal are an integral part of the business planning cycle. Many local authorities and housing associations have some form of performance appraisal. Tying this more closely to objectives and strategies will allow it to be integrated into a business planning cycle. This will then provide a basis on which to consider the next round of planning.

How will we know whether we are getting there?

You can only monitor how you are doing if you:

- Know where you want to be

    — i.e. you have clear objectives and strategies about how to meet those objectives

    — forecasts of how quickly you expect to implement the strategies which will meet your objectives

- Have a monitoring programme

    — which evaluates progress against your expectations

    — which indicates in advance when you need to amend your strategies

    — tells you when your objectives may need to be revised

Sources of Information

Further Reading

1. *Exploring Corporate Strategy*
   G. Johnson and K. Scholes
   (Prentice Hall 1989)

2. *Business Policy*
   G. Luffman, S. Sanderson, E. Lea, B. Kenny
   (Basil Blackwell 1989)

3. *Practical Corporate Planning*
   J. Argenti
   (Routledge 1991)

4. *Designing Organizations*
   R. Butler
   (Routledge 1991)

5. *The Art of Managing Finance*
   D. Davies
   (McGraw-Hill 1985)

6. *Accounting for Management Control*
   C. Emmanuel, D. Otley, K. Merchant
   (Chapman and Hall 1990)

7. *Managing Housing Budgets in a Competitive Environment*
   D. Garland and J. Parker
   (Longman / Chartered Institute of Housing 1993)

8. *Marketing Management*
   R. Kotler
   (Prentice Hall 1988)

9. *Housing Management Standards Manual*
   (Chartered Institute of Housing 1993)

10. *CCT and Local Authority Housing*
    (Association of District Councils/Chartered Institute of Housing 1993)

11. *Redefining Housing Association Business Plans*
    (Scottish Homes 1994)

12. *Business Planning for Small Housing Associations*
    (National Federation of Housing Associations 1993)

13. *Paying the Piper*
    (Audit Commission 1995)

14. *Calling the Tune*
    (Audit Commission 1995)

15. *Trusting in the Future*
    (Audit Commission 1994)